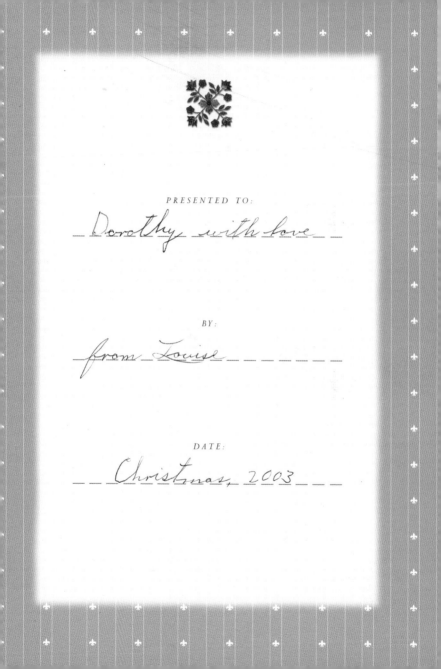

PRESENTED TO:

Dorothy with love

BY:

from Louise

DATE:

Christmas, 2003

QUILTED WITH LOVE

Discovering the Patterns of Life's Grace and Beauty.

Debbie Salter Goodwin

Quilted with Love
ISBN 1-56292-781-7
Copyright © 2001 by Debbie Salter Goodwin
Published by
Honor Books
P. O. Box 55388
Tulsa, Oklahoma 74155

Design and production by Koechel Peterson & Associates,
Minneapolis, Minnesota

Printed in Hong Kong.

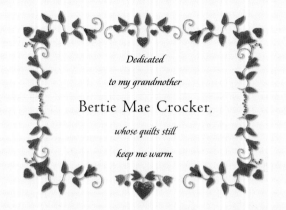

Dedicated

to my grandmother

Bertie Mae Crocker,

whose quilts still

keep me warm.

Acknowledgments

No book is a singular work. Many people coauthor with the person whose name appears in the byline. Here are some of the people I wish to thank for their indispensable contributions: To Renette, thank you for the retreat theme that grew into a book. To my editor, Rebecca Currington, thank you for making my "stitches" tighter in this quilt pattern of words and images. To my husband Mark and daughter Lisa, thank you for listening to each new draft with such affirming willingness. And to those of you who shared your quilts and their stories with me, you are the essence of all that follows.

Introduction

Quilts are storytellers—remnants of life pieced together in beautiful patterns that speak of baby bonnets and Easter dresses, bathroom curtains and Christmas tree skirts. They help us picture relatives we have never met. They teach us about patience and friendship, tradition and heritage while they cover our beds, our chairs, and the people we love. As a whole, they help define us by holding in trust our most cherished memories.

Even if you are not a quilter, you have probably snuggled under the warmth and weight of one of these wonderful creations. And you may well have come to appreciate the remarkable versatility of a quilt, whether stacked in a closet waiting for company, spread out under a tree to accommodate a picnic, hung on a wall, or draped across a bed. And who could fail to see their value as precious heirlooms, some carefully packed away, too precious to use. Whatever you do with a quilt, it always adds beauty, warmth, creativity, and memories to your life.

In the pages that follow, some of the quilts I've known tell their stories and share their lessons. I invite you to open your heart and listen. Somewhere there is a pattern of truth stitched just for you.

Debbie Salter Goodwin

TABLE OF CONTENTS

A QUILTER'S PRAYER

Take the pieces of my life
And stitch them together
According to Your will.

May I yield to the pricks of Your needle
so that Your stitches
may surround me with the pattern of Your love.

May I allow You to order the squares
any way You want,
To pattern me by Your design
So that all will know
You quilted me.

PART I

PIECES

Life, like a quilt, creates something new
by rearranging the pieces.

PIECES

Gather the pieces that are left over. Let nothing be wasted.

JOHN 6:12

Cleaning out the sewing closet, she found them—folded lengths of outdated fabric purchased for projects never begun and remnants of the clothes she no longer wore. As her fingers touched the pieces, she dreamed of other times: sewing lessons with her grandmother; making her first doll clothes; dresses she watched her mother make with all the fittings, handwork, and pressing. Halloween costumes, doll clothes, baby dresses, place mats—the list was endless. These pieces bore witness to weddings and funerals, church and picnics.

On the shelf in the sewing closet, they collect dust. But in a quilt, the folded fabric takes on new meaning. Squares of life, like a scrapbook, opening yesterday and reminding us that our lives come from God. Reminding us that beauty isn't limited by age or restricted by fashion.

It is quilting theology. God takes the pieces of our lives and stitches them together, working His will for the good of those who love Him. With His handiwork, life isn't limited to one square. It is a pattern of squares where beauty depends on variety and no single square tells the whole story. They must be seen together—like a quilt.

Dear God,

Protect me from responding to pieces of my life
as the whole story. It is the same as treating pieces of the
truth as the whole truth. Help me to
understand that nothing need be wasted when stitched
together by Your will. I offer You my
gathered pieces to be stitched together for Your purpose.
Amen.

I THINK GOD
IS A QUILTER

I think God is a quilter
Who takes His needle and thread
To piece our world from nothingness
And give it form, instead.

I think God is a quilter
And everything I see
Are pieces from His careful hand
From tree to bumblebee.

I think we see God's stitches
His texture everywhere;
The velvet moss, the grainy sand,
The silky strands of hair.

I think God is a quilter;
Stitching tight and tiny rows,
Adding to my scraps and pieces,
Seaming everything He knows.

I think He cuts the patterns
From what I'd throw away.
He shows me how to use each scrap
In His redeeming way.

I think God quilts a pattern
From everything I live;
But He can only stitch the quilt
From what I choose to give.

I think God is a quilter
Stitching strength where I am weak.
Showing me that life He touches
Embraces everything I seek.

I think God is a quilter
From the patience in each thread;
Proving length of time no barrier;
Treating time a gift, instead.

I think quilts are lessons
God uses just to teach
That our pieces and our remnants
Have kaleidoscopic reach.

So, in the life I'm living
With pieces everywhere
I'll give them to the Quilter
To stitch with loving care.

I'll give them to the Quilter
Unwanted though they be
And with His work of quilting
He'll make a quilt of me.

THE WEDDING QUILT

A gift opens the way for the giver.

PROVERBS 18:16

I t was in the attic, a long-forgotten keepsake from her great grandmother. The family had always called it a sampler. To her great grandmother, it was a wedding quilt, named for the occasion for which it was made.

The wedding quilt was a community tradition back then. When a couple married, the women of the community would meet to piece together a quilt for the young bride. It was a practical gift. Every home needed covering for the beds.

Each woman chose a pattern and material pieces to make the sampler. As she did, each square became a personal gift of her own creativity. Perhaps it was also prophetic of the different patterns the bride's new life would hold, each square a sampling of what was to come.

As the women met to stitch the squares, they stitched themselves together, too, offering pieces of friendship as they talked of births and deaths, children and husbands, crops and canning, hopes and disappointments. The quilt was not about remnants. It was about life. And the gift they gave was not as great as the gift they received in the quilting.

As Mikayla unfolded the wedding quilt, she thought of the young women she knew. It would take more than a quilt to bring them together. So many had been touched by hurt and separation. But she remembered her great grandmother saying that quilting was also a way to break the daily routine and share burdens. The quilts they produced did more than warm a bed; they quilted hearts together with love. *How many "quilting sessions" need to happen over coffee cups or through phone calls, baby-sitting swaps, and encouragement cards,* she wondered.

Mikayla brought her great grandmother's wedding quilt down from the attic to lay folded at the end of the guest bed. But its lesson exposed her need. In a culture that praises the individual, she felt individually isolated. Tracing the stitches with her finger, she longed for a circle of women who would nurture her with relationships.

Didn't her great grandmother's quilt start with a need and an invitation? Perhaps the young women she knew needed to learn a new kind of quilting, the kind that quilts hearts instead of fabric squares. *Perhaps we could learn together,* she thought as she reached for the phone.

Dear God,

Help me quilt myself to other women

who need the connection as much as I do.

Protect me from the sterility and isolation

that our society would impose

with electronic communication

that cannot hug away a hurt or share a smile.

May I learn the lesson of the wedding quilt

and add my patterned block to another

person's life only to find her pattern

neatly stitched into mine.

Amen.

PIECES OF LOVE

Lord, the one you love is sick.

JOHN 11:3

Her friends wanted to send her a piece of themselves, so they made her a quilt. With great love, they stitched, embroidered, or painted a comforting Bible verse beside their family names. Then, those who knew how sewed the pieces together with her favorite navy blue. They meant it as a bold reminder of the love link that distance or even cancer could not affect.

When the quilt arrived, Kay asked that it be hung on the wall opposite her hospital bed. It was a love letter she could read each morning after radiation or chemotherapy. The quilt reminded her that she was not alone—not ever. Even when her breaths came harder and the pain more often, the quilt was there and so was every person who contributed a square.

She talked about the quilt and the people who made it with nurses and doctors and volunteers. People made special trips to her room to see the quilt. It was not the craftsmanship that impressed them. It was the love.

So, it was only right that when Kay died, this quilt of love covered the casket as it had covered her life. No spray of flowers could have been as beautiful as this multi-squared original. No words spoken could have been as encouraging as this comforter of love. It was a cold reality that death could take one so young in the beginnings of marriage and motherhood. Only love could soften such harshness.

The love quilt no longer reminds of death, for there is a lot of life stitched into each pattern: hers and theirs. Now, bequeathed to the daughter who must finish her mother's love story, the quilt still comforts and strengthens with gentle memories and reminds us that life is a priceless treasure.

Dear God,

Remind me often that two things can never die:

prayer and love. The prayers we pray for others

wrap them in peace and comfort them like a warm quilt.

They are tangible evidence of the love we share with them.

Amen.

MISS LILLY'S QUILT

If I have found favor in your eyes, accept this gift from me.

GENESIS 33:10

They called her Miss Lilly in true Southern style. She was a neighbor who lived down the street in her own world of fabricated reality. Such is the address of the developmentally disabled, and Miss Lilly was that. Everyone knew. They said it ran in the family. It was mild enough to allow her a kind of independent life, yet it was obvious to all that she was different.

Somehow Miss Lilly managed to take care of the simple things of life. No one really knew how. She looked neither sickly nor abandoned. So what was it that identified her as different? Her disheveled appearance, perhaps, or her haphazard clothing choices? Maybe it was the way she talked to herself as she walked down the street or a look in her eyes that told you she saw the world through a different set of spectacles.

What was obvious or common sense to everyone else translated as mystery to Miss Lilly. She could buy groceries, but she couldn't make change. She could sweep a floor with the religious commitment of a saint and live with cluttered stacks in every room of her house. She could dress herself but not in combinations that matched. Mostly she kept to herself, which was the way the neighborhood liked it.

It wasn't until Marla, a young woman who lived down the street, was expecting a baby that Miss Lilly ventured out to connect with the expectant mother.

"You expectin' a baby, I see." Miss Lilly patted the bulge beneath Marla's dress.

"Why, yes I am. In July."

"I'd like to make a quilt for your baby," Miss Lilly said with a smile so confident that the mother-to-be had to believe that this simple lady could, in fact, complete this mission, though she might seriously wonder what it would look like. The hands that had touched her belly were not the hands of a careful seamstress. They shook. They did nothing gently. What would they do to pieces of fabric? What would they do with a needle in hand? What difference did it make? The woman wanted to make a gift. There is no need for quality control when someone wants to give a gift.

"That would be fine."

And then this unlikely giver began with great authority to announce a list of supplies that Marla should buy: the fabric, the thread, the batting, the backing. At least the woman could repeat the ingredients necessary for quilt-making. But could she quilt? Time would tell. Out of respect for Miss Lilly's kindness to her, Marla bought the material and other needed supplies. She selected blue gingham and a blue print.

Miss Lilly called every day to give her a progress report. First, she had cut the squares. Then, she had pieced them. Every step of this process she chronicled with a phone call. It proved to be a connection that soon could almost be called a friendship. Not only did the two women talk about the quilt and its process but the baby or the events of the day or a favorite recipe. They were never long interchanges, and Marla always supplied the questions, while Miss Lilly gave her answers in spurts.

The young mother-to-be came to depend on this

daily interchange the same way she marked her day by laundry and meals and cleanup. It became such a part of her that something was missing without a phone call from Miss Lilly.

Finally, several weeks before the baby was born, Miss Lilly called with the announcement, "Well, I finished it. I'd like to bring it over sometime."

"I'm looking forward to seeing it," Marla answered.

Just a couple of minutes later, there was a knock at the door, and an excited Miss Lilly reported, "Here it is. I couldn't wait." She pulled the quilt from a shopping bag as though it were an heirloom to be passed to another generation. With great ceremony and the sparkle of pride in her eyes, Miss Lilly brushed the quilt tenderly with the palm of her hand. Marla didn't have to look at the quilt to know it was a thing of beauty to Miss Lilly.

The unfolded quilt revealed permanently bunched stitches pinching fabric in their irregular grip. Nothing was straight or uniform—not the quilting stitches or the cut-out squares. Scattered generously throughout were a mass of knots where the thread had hopelessly tangled and Miss Lilly had simply kept on stitching. She saw none of these imperfections.

— — — —

In a way, neither did Marla. Of course she knew they were there, but they did not mar the gift in her mind. She saw them through her daily phone calls from Miss Lilly. She saw them as a picture of Miss Lilly's own life, pieces stitched together with bunches and tangles. She saw them as the measure of Miss Lilly's courage—a courage she would soon need in her life as she prepared for labor and parenting.

That's when the transformation of Miss Lilly's quilt began. As Marla saw the gift through eyes of love, she no longer saw the imperfections. They had become the artwork of love, unique and singular.

The baby came. They named her Amanda. She was their treasure—perfect, by her parents' measure, even though she did nothing on time or by convenience. She complicated their schedules, robbed them of sleep, and knotted their hearts with her unconditional acceptance— just like Miss Lilly had done.

At first the quilt was treated as a masterpiece, set apart and too precious to use. Other quilts wrapped Amanda in a different kind of beauty as she went to church. A handmade afghan draped over her crib. Cross-stitched crib quilts covered the sleeping angel at night, and Miss Lilly's quilt waited.

It was when Amanda was old enough to grasp and recognize a thing for what it was that Miss Lilly's quilt left its shelf and made trips with the baby. Amanda would take a corner of the quilt in one hand and suck her thumb with the other. Soon, the quilt was a constant companion. She never left the house without it. The quilt went in her stroller to the shopping mall. It went in the shopping cart at the grocery store. When Amanda began walking, she dragged it behind her like a pull-toy. She sat on it, napped on it, ate with it. Next to her mother and father, Miss Lilly's quilt was her closest companion.

Unlike the other artifacts of infancy, the quilt out-lived toys and stuffed bears, even dolls. It accompanied Amanda to school and waited for reunion afterwards. Permanently stained, threadbare, coming apart at the seams, still Miss Lilly's quilt was Amanda's favorite.

Until high school, that is. It wasn't that Amanda grew too old for the quilt, but her friends were simply too young to understand the meaning of this old friend. So Amanda took to hiding the quilt in the trunk of the car when she went to school—not because she was embarrassed by it but to protect the quilt from teasing, like her mother had protected Miss Lilly, accepting her within her context and not asking her to travel outside of it.

Amanda went off to college without Miss Lilly's quilt. She no longer needed the familiar companion in hand to connect to its meaning. Her mother keeps it in the upstairs linen closet just outside the room that belongs to Amanda whenever she comes home. One day, Miss Lilly's quilt will take a journey with Amanda into another level of independence.

The quilt will teach Amanda that love is a priceless gift; that expressions of love are as unique as every stitch in Miss Lilly's quilt; that to receive love, it is often necessary to see the gift from the heart of the giver; that imperfections from a heart of love create their own beauty. Miss Lilly's quilt, like Miss Lilly herself, outlived everyone's expectations. She made a life for herself and a quilt for Amanda, both rich with meaning and texture.

O God,

Teach me to know the richness of a gift

by looking at the heart of the giver.

Help me to receive love freely

and place no quality standards on it.

Help me realize that all of us have

our knots and tangles.

Some of us simply hide them better.

Amen.

THE SCHOOL
PROJECT QUILT

*It is to be a witness between us and
you and the generations.*

JOSHUA 22:27

She needed a fifth-grade school project about her home state: Georgia. She wanted to do something unusual and unique. And she wanted a good grade.

A notebook! Annie thought. *A carefully organized, thoroughly researched notebook.* She could get pictures, divide it into sections, make it thick and colorful. Then, her imagination glimpsed turn-in day, and she saw the stack of notebooks on her teacher's desk. A notebook would not be unusual and unique even if it were thick and colorful.

What about a song? She could incorporate Georgia history into every phrase and stanza. She imagined a song so compelling that even the governor would agree that it should replace the state song. But suddenly, the choir singing in her head stopped mid-quarter-note. There was a problem. She couldn't write music.

Annie followed her mother around as she went about the day's tasks and asked for ideas.

"Sounds like you need something new and fresh to cover the subject without being boring," her mother offered as she smoothed the night lines from the quilts to make the bed. "What about a quilt?"

"A quilt?" Her daughter wrinkled her nose and squinted her eyes, trying to see the quilt in her mind as clearly as she had visualized her other ideas. But no image came.

"I don't know the first thing about making a quilt," she fretted.

"No. But Grandma does," her mother reminded her.

The idea took shape square by square. Annie's mother helped her purchase the material for the blocks, binding, and backing. It would be almost like a note-book, except that the pages would be sewn together rather than hole-punched.

They chose a Sunday afternoon to put the quilt together. Three generations of Georgians—grandmother, mother, and daughter. How they put the quilt together mirrored their lives in more ways than they realized.

— — — —

Ten-year-old Annie had done all the research. After all, it was her project and her grade. She had identified the state tree, the state flower, the state bird, even the state insect. She found the pictures she wanted to reproduce. Learning is always a first-person process, an adventure of discovery. Shortcuts always shortchange. Even when the research is confusing or tedious, there is no substitute for doing the work yourself. It is a life lesson Annie was ready to learn.

Annie's mother cut the squares and traced the pictures onto the blocks, creating the pattern her daughter could fill in with permanent markers. It felt like a natural function for a mother—supplying patterns and outlines for her child as personality and interests began to emerge, setting protective boundaries to prevent destructive influences, praying arduous prayers as she made a permanent mark within the patterns she had chosen. To be willing to sketch the patterns and transfer to her child the responsibility for choosing and filling the squares is the most painful lesson of motherhood. To have the wisdom to recognize the right pattern is the ongoing lesson of maturity. But mother nor daughter thought of the larger lesson as they enjoyed working together on the quilt.

Annie's grandmother sat at the sewing machine and stitched the blocks together. It takes generational wisdom to put pieces of life together. It takes a perspective that youth cannot achieve. Asking Grandmother to use her long experience at a sewing machine to stitch the squares together for a school project is somehow easier than asking her to teach you what life choices protected her from, or caused, the pain of regret.

The quilt became an umbilical cord to birth something that had nothing to do with school or grades. For in the process of their work, they laughed and told stories and encouraged each other. They overlapped their lives, pattern on pattern and love on love in ways that melted away the differences of age.

They backed the quilt with a pink bandanna print—not especially Georgian, but definitely fifth-grade girl. Finished, the quilt made a visual statement no other report would make. And Annie was very proud.

In a sense, all three went to school the day the quilt was due: grandmother, mother, and daughter. However, only the daughter was marked present. She had done it, created a unique and unusual project. The quilt was applauded by everyone in the class, and it so impressed the teacher that she hung it in the school hall for several weeks.

Three generations worked together on history they did not create. Three generations cut, sewed, traced. Three generations together without a gap or debate. They were quilted together. The school project quilt proved that age makes a difference, not a distance.

Hanging on the wall, the quilt taught school children about Georgia. Remembering the Sunday afternoon marathon, the quilt taught three generations about life.

Dear God,

Teach me that age is a continuity thread to bind us together. Help me see that differences add texture and do not need to separate. How I need the wisdom of age and the optimism of youth. I understand that to live without a gap between generations, I must be the bridge.

Show me where to start.

Amen.

THE IRONING-BOARD QUILT

We boast about your perseverance.

2 THESSALONIANS 1:4

"Lordy, it's old." Jewellene, the daughter of the ironing-board carver spoke the truth. She spoke it in the rhythm of her people. Her Southern speech could string words together like pearls. Her voice was a mix of pitch and drawl, still vibrant with experience and not simply age. Her skin was smooth as porcelain and translucent as waxed paper.

Jewellene, a name you must lean into both by accent and delight. A name as Southern as her birthright. A name that fit this jewel, not by reference to an expensive price tag but because true jewels keep their worth no matter the setting.

The ironing board was also a jewel but not because of its price tag or setting. It was old, much older than Jewellene. For that, Jewellene was most grateful. At a hundred years old, it was older than anyone in the room. Since beauty acquires new definition with age, this ironing board no longer hid its flaws. It wore them as testimony to its antique status.

The granddaughter of the board carver hung the ironing board on the wall of her kitchen, not for easy access but for memories. The years robbed her of many memories, but the presence of the old ironing board placed a few close enough to touch. That was the whole idea behind hanging it on the wall.

"Why don't you throw that old thing away?" her sister advised. She had no use for something so old, not an ironing board or the memories attached to it. But Jewellene was glad that one of her daughters had a place for it.

Jewellene's daddy had carved the board, and her mamma had covered it with an old quilt. The quilt made a good ironing-board pad to launch flatirons and send them sailing across broadcloth or taffeta. This had been a three-iron house. If you kept the rhythm right, you always had a hot iron ready. Like braiding, it had been important to remember which iron you used last.

There was a smell to ironing in those days that didn't come from spray starch or fabric softener. The stoked wood fire from the cooking stove heated the flatirons. Heated metal added an acrid odor to the room. Press hot metal to cotton, and there was the roasted fiber smell like a campfire stick.

Since the flatiron had no protective heel rests, it had to wait on the ironing board or on the cookstove. Left too long on the board, it scorched the cover. Add to this the fact that a flatiron heated on a wood stove must be rubbed clean to remove its smoky film, and the quilt had little chance. The black hieroglyphics and dark bruises eventually obliterated any remaining color and pattern. Scorched to brown, the stitches and pins no longer held it together. The material simply melted until the board wore the quilt as a graft.

The quilt cover accepted these burns and bruises into its very fiber, permanently marking it for the rest of its life. Only one square of the quilt had managed to retain its color.

"The Jewellene Square I call it," her daughter remarked. And rightly so because Jewellene is as much a survivor as the ironing-board quilt. The rocks and knocks of her life so scorched her fraying pieces, that she could have become nothing more than a blackened remnant to be hidden or stored. Instead, she walks with regal beauty in spite of her muscles' lethargy from a recent stroke, and her eyes spark with mischief and story.

"When Hugh and I married, his mother couldn't iron," Jewellene remarked once. "So when we moved in with his mother, I did the ironing. Hugh's brothers admired his crisp, scorch-free shirts. And I was proud that I could iron better than any of them. So they began bringing me their shirts, then their pants. I could put a very professional looking crease in pants. That was in the day of BJ stretchers. You didn't just hang pants out to dry; you inserted pant stretchers. They hung like cardboard cut-outs of half a man.

"I don't know why I sweated over the ironing on those steamy Georgia days. I guess I wanted them to like me, so I did what they liked me to do—until I learned better. Then, I told them they should take their shirts and pants to the laundry if they wanted them pressed. You know what they say, live and learn—or just live."

Like Jewellene, the quilt just lives—not as a eulogy to the once bright and patterned cover that showcased a bed. The quilt lives to testify that scorch marks do not mar life or hide beauty. The pieces that show through speak the loudest. Jewellene has many pieces like that. When looking at those pieces, others don't see the ugly scorches where people rubbed their darkness onto her life. She smiles the smile of a survivor. It is the only piece of her life we need to see.

Dear God,

What piece of my life shows through the years?

What part of me perseveres?

When I am scorched and marked,

will I still show beauty

like the ironing-board quilt?

If You design the piece, I will wear the scar.

Amen.

QUILTS RECYCLE LIFE

*We know that in all things God works for
the good of those who love him.*

ROMANS 8:28

Quilts

Recycle life in more ways than one.

Taking pieces of color

Scraps from yesterday

They are stitched together

To create a pattern from discards.

The quilt spreads the truth that nothing need be wasted, not the crazy pattern and outdated colors, not the yardage bought on whim and never used, not the dark pieces nor the ones too small for anything else.

In a quilt

Everything works for beauty.

Everything works for good.

Perhaps God's work in my life is more like piecing a quilt than painting a picture.

— — — —

For it is only pieces that I have to give;

    some dark and ugly,

    some crazy cutouts,

    some small,

    some bright,

    some costly,

    some so precious I can hardly stand to part with them,

So instead of taking pieces of my life remnants to a trash pile

He pieces them;

Stitches them into a beautiful pattern

Where dark neighbors light,

Where small is big enough,

Where memories are preserved.

And everything works for beauty;

Everything works for good.

A BAG OF PIECES

How many . . . broken pieces did you collect?

MARK 8:19 NRSV

Her life was in pieces. Scraps of her childhood lay before her like knocked-over garbage. And now a new piece had been added to the chaos. She was pregnant—unmarried and pregnant; maybe even unloved and pregnant, although she didn't want to explore that possibility right now. For her, there would be no celebration announcement, only whispers and morning sickness. She took a long, gray look into a future where her dreams would never come true—not now.

"I'm no mother," Sandi confessed. "No matter what the biological capability of my body may be, I can't raise a child. Not now, anyway." Besides, she didn't want this baby to inherit the history of her own abuse and dysfunction. She took this new piece of life, even before it was brought from her body, and gave it up. She wanted more than she had wanted anything for this piece to be treated better than the other scraps of her history. She signed the papers for her baby to be

46

adopted. She endured the agony of separation and silence through the years.

This separation also haunted Sandi's daughter. Adoption gave her a family, but it was a borrowed identity. She clutched it, almost fearfully. She had a name and family tree, but it did not connect her with a bloodline. How much identity had she missed because she did not know her birth mother? Over and over, she took out this piece about her life and studied it. But letting one piece of life substitute for the whole is no answer. It provides little comfort and even less truth.

Many times, Sandi thought about this daughter, a piece of her life that was sewn into someone else's pattern. All the while, her life grew over the hole in her heart from which this piece came. Time was her friend, and she began to make something new of the pieces.

Sandi learned that scraps, if cut into geometric shapes and sewn together, create a certain kind of beauty out of diversity. She was almost addicted to the process of making quilt squares. Was it because she wanted to know that the odd pieces of her life could belong somewhere as well? Was she tired of blaming ragged scraps for so much unhappiness? Or was it her prayer that the piece of her life she had given away was providing beauty in another pattern? Whatever drove her to the pieces, she meticulously cut and stitched and filled a sack.

There they remained, these blocks of print and color. The hard part was finished, or was it? Was that what she had done with her life? Blocked pieces and stuffed them away. There were the unfinished relationships she had walked away from, the dreams she had given up on, the jobs that never panned out. *Surely,* she reasoned, *my life amounts to more than a bag of unfinished pieces.*

That day her life changed. Really it was more than a day. She wrote and mailed a letter, asking if the daughter was willing to make contact with her birth mother, willing to bring this piece to center focus.

They met, mother and daughter, both now from separate worlds, their forgotten umbilical connection adding little to make this awkward meeting comfortable. They touched the pieces of their torn-apart lives until they found one place of similarity—quilting.

"I quilted once," Sandi said in response to her daughter's inquiry. "I mean, I started a quilt. The pieces are still in a sack somewhere in the closet."

"I'd love to see them," her daughter coaxed.

Soon Sandi was bringing out a sack and showing her daughter the colorful squares, confessing that she would probably never finish it. "Maybe you would like them?" she asked. Was it the child putting the mother together? Or was it the mother's last chance to see something that she had made come together into a whole instead of remaining in pieces?

The meeting ended with a promise to return when the quilt was complete. Sandi took pride in her daughter, the piece of her life that had grown whole and happy somewhere else. She no longer saw her life in pieces but in patterned parts only time could stitch into a whole. She knew one day a quilt would come from the sack of pieces just as a lovely young woman had come from the bundle that had gone with the papers she signed. Maybe now the other pieces of her life would come together as well. And maybe she would let them. No more scraps. Beauty waited in the pieces.

Sandi's daughter took the pieces home, put needle to thread and threaded needle to piece. She re-backed and re-stitched. Soon she realized that the quilt she was working on was a lot like the life this woman had given her—just pieces, nothing whole. Possibilities needing to be stitched together in love. Her birth mother had taken the first stitch, but there had been many more stitches since then. She saw them now, the birthday stitches, the sickbed stitches, the shared-tear stitches. They were stitches that made her belong where she had been pieced. Suddenly, she saw that identity is not a one-source issue. Looking at her adoption and comparing it to the piece called family, she found that the source of her life did not predict or prevent as much as she thought.

Both mother and daughter had learned the truth of pieces—that a piece is not the whole; that love stitches more identity than genes; and that wholeness happens when the pieces are in the right place. A finished quilt would remind them both that the pieces were in the right place.

God,

Where I have treated a piece as the whole,

forgive me.

Where I need to learn where the pieces fit,

teach me.

Where I need to finish what I started,

encourage me.

Amen.

PART II

PATTERNS

*Patterns create design with distance
and beauty with time.*

THE SAMPLER

Surely I have a delightful inheritance.

PSALM 16:6

The sampler quilt covers my bed in the same way my mother covered my life. Her gathered experiences pieced together a sample of life in which she offered me lessons about faith and faithfulness that I did not have to learn the hard way.

Perhaps it was learning to take life's leftovers and make something useful with them that pressed her to make the quilt. Even the quilting process was a lesson in life. It treated life stages as separate squares to seam together, carefully and tightly. The stages created a picture, and the picture spoke of life.

In many ways, the sampler squares marked her life stages. The square called "Steps to the Altar" described the wedding that made her a wife and eventually a mother. Did the steps warn that dreams do not come true just because of a marriage vow? Did they remind that there were steps to growing a dream or that some of the steps might be harder than others?

There was "Grandmother's Flower Garden" on the quilt and in the backyard. My grandmother lived with us. She was resident grandmother for the two of us girls and later my brother. She always had a garden: gladiolas, periwinkles, poppies, coleus, and the elephant ears we used as shields in our pretend play. There never was a manicured lawn artistically landscaped. But there were always flowers and, Grandmother was the only one who grew them.

The "Star and Crescent" square reminded me of the many moons and twinkles that filled the night skies over the years. It consisted of darkness broken by pieces of light. Life had its darkness: neurosurgery for my three-month-old brother and my mother's numerous surgeries and health concerns. But there were also many pieces of light. It is always true that contrast produces its own beauty.

The "Wonder of the World" square incorporated a visit to Niagara Falls and a trip to the Grand Canyon. It spoke of redwoods and the painted desert, seeing the country from sea to shining sea as my mother and father traveled on business and for pleasure. There were many wonders, each a different pattern, each a different beauty, each pointing to a Designer who understood that diversity creates unmatched beauty and awesome wonder.

My fingers continue to trace the patterns. The "Dresden Plate" is next. Was this a dream for a fine-china life instead of the metallic-flecked melmac that defined the family table? Did she save parts of herself like she saved her china? If mother taught us anything, she taught us that there is a time for china and a time for melmac. Joy comes from knowing what time it is.

The "Honey Bee" design of swirls and patches tells the story of one who searches for sweetness and beauty and drinks deeply with each discovery. My mother could always find that beauty. She taught us to drink in sunsets and snowscapes. She gloried in butterflies and bluebonnets. I learned from her that anyone who looks for beauty and sweetness will find it.

The "Eight-Pointed Star" was for the Texas years. The first furtive steps of marriage, family, career were all sometimes very isolated and lonely in their beginnings. Yet, her beginnings shone with star-like brightness.

Married to a man addicted to travel and back-tonature camping, it is no surprise that my mother's sampler quilt had a "Log Cabin" square. Thankfully for all of us, we only moved to a cabin in the woods for vacation. I have come to understand it was a negotiated compromise.

"Tippecanoe" may memorialize an Indian war, but for our family it will always remind us of the canoe trip when we almost toppled over the falls. Dad was an explorer. He wanted to investigate the rushing sound in the distance. Moments before the current would have pulled us into the rush of water and plunged us over the rock cliff, he realized it was a waterfall he was hearing. Some fierce paddling returned us to the lazy glide we had been enjoying.

A sampler quilt. A beginner's practice run. The quilt tells the story of life in squares because life is a sampler, combining joy and sorrow side by side just like the different patterns of a quilt. Except life is not a practice.

Would life be easier if it were more like a sampler quilt and we could flip through a pattern book for the squares we wanted to live? Would we have picked the grief square from which we learned trust? Would we have selected the darkness from which we learned the source of light? Would we have chosen hard times from which we learned strength? No. It is the sampler that we need.

The sampler quilt is the story of my mother's life and lessons bequeathed. In times when I must work on a painful square that seems to have no place in my dream, I look at her quilt and relax.

Dear God,

Let me not fear the sampler squares

that invite me to taste

the multi-textured life

You know is best for me.

And when the square is not of my choosing,

let me see the beauty You make

of the choice I always have:

to accept it as a sample of life.

Amen.

BORDERS

I will establish your borders.

EXODUS 23:31

S he took her newest quilt to show her oldest friend. They talked of family and past joys and quilting. "This is my ninth quilt," Jean informed her. The quilt was a work of art, though it was destined for a bed. "This is my first," her friend Esther confessed, before bringing out the patchwork quilt she had made for her daughter-in-law.

"Now that it's almost finished, she wants me to make it king-sized," Esther whispered. "But I don't know how. Would you help me?" she asked.

There was irony in this simple question. Years before, these women had met when Jean, a young wife and mother, had asked Esther for help. She needed a voice of experience as she worked to get her young family settled in a new town.

Jean, the wife of a loan officer at a large insurance company, was looking for a job. Esther, the wife of a minister who had administrative responsibility over pastors, knew her husband was looking for a secretary. A phone call connected them the first time. Esther called Jean as a favor to a mutual friend. That contact was casual and helpful in a surface way. However, the years would prove this more than a chance meeting. It was a border in the making.

The minister hired Jean to work at home long before job-sharing and home offices were popular. And when Jean's young husband decided to answer God's call to pastor, the same employer-minister gave the loan officer his first church. The border continued to grow.

One Christmas, funds were tight at the newly organized church and at home. Jean and her husband knew that their personal funds would decorate only one tree, so they decided that it would be the church tree. Without complaint, they bought the bubble lights, the twisted foil garland, the red velvet rope, the metallic balls, and of course, icicles. When Esther learned of her young friend's sacrifice, she acted like any mother would. She bought decorations for the church tree and sent the "borrowed" decorations back home where they belonged. In that moment when compassion met an uncovered need, the border broadened and the edges were finished with love.

From this event came a relationship not based simply on employment or pastoral accountability. The more experienced couple modeled and mentored. They were always ready with advice and encouragement. Each time they encouraged their young friends, they stitched a pattern filled with possibility into the pieces of their lives.

We all need border friends—people who stand at the edges of our lives and help us see what we cannot when we are trying to place the pieces of life into meaningful patterns. They are people who come alongside with truth, honesty, and encouragement—in that order. They are people who see in us what we cannot see in ourselves. They are people who, by their bordering, help make us what we did not know we could be. Such is the work of a border.

Jean finished the border for her friend. It was a simple job for an experienced quilter. She took it back to the woman who had shared so much with her. It was a humble trade. An offer for payment was absolutely refused.

Payment? Jean thought. *For what?* She had only added a few stitches in some places. It was both gift and privilege to take a few hours to enjoy her friend's creation. *I should be paying her,* she thought, almost out loud. And she remembered the borders, the wisdom, the growing-edge counsel, the turning points, the job changes, the crisis compassion. It was a long border that reached all the way around her adult life and embraced her with transparent love.

Was it simply coincidence or the unmistakable timing of God that prompted Jean to deliver the newly bordered quilt just days before a fall left Esther in a coma? In the days of slow recovery, Jean took her turn sitting beside her friend in border reversal.

It is the way of friendship to border each other— to stand sentinel, ready to help or give silent support. To be a friend is to be a border. It is the border that makes us see the beauty of pattern. It is the border, often plain and simple, that completes a picture.

It took Jean only a couple of weeks to finish the border for the patchwork quilt. But the border Esther stitched around Jean's life took more than forty-eight years. Both are works of art.

— — — —

*God, border me
with those who will finish off
my rough edges. May I never reject truth
in any form, even if it requires
unstitching pieces to put my pattern
together again. I submit my life,
with all its pieces and patterns,
to be bordered.
Amen.*

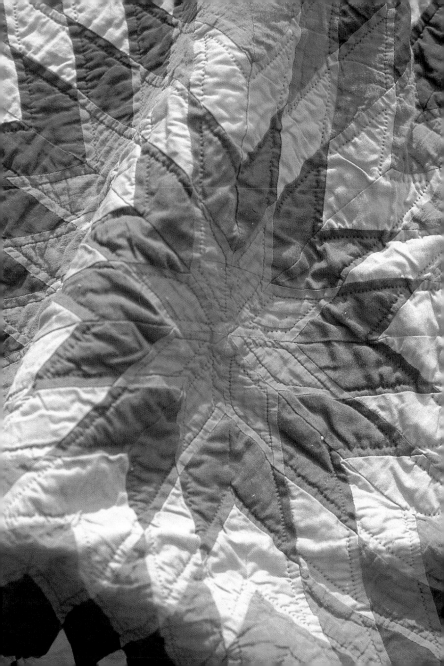

GRANDMOTHER'S QUILT

Age should speak; advanced years should teach wisdom.

JOB 32:7

S he still remembers making the selections for the fabric that would bind the quilt together. It was a popular color scheme making a comeback today—a blend of avocado green and citrus orange. Her grandmother had promised to make each of her granddaughters a quilt, pieced together from all the clothes she had helped make for them through the years. And so, in a way, the quilt became the story of Marla's life.

There was the pink linen and lace formal she had worn to the spring banquet at college, the one where she announced the engagement that would not lead to marriage. Another square held the sky-blue velvet from the first time she was a bridesmaid. And how could she forget the leopard fake-fur vest she had so proudly worn. It was as close as she would ever get to the Age of Aquarius! Making her wardrobe was a cost-cutting necessity for a college girl.

Marla's grandmother made everything fit into the quilt. While the squares were uniformly three and one-half by three and one-half, she used triangles and strips of every size to piece them. Color coordination was not as great a concern for her as the memories. So gold satin lay beside lime polyester and navy, turquoise, and pastel blue marched together as if they had come from the same bolt.

The quilt tells the story of a grandmother's love and patience. Day after day, she cut and pinned and sewed. Having never attended a quilting class, she laid the squares on her bed to check for size and placement. Marla wasn't sure how long it took her grandmother to finish the quilt. She only knew that when she put it on her bed for the first time, she was as proud of it as if she had made it herself.

It was her quilt—hand made from her grandmother's heart, stitched with love and bordered with prayer. While it would never win a quilting prize, it would always have first place in Marla's heart. Her quilt gave her more than a scrapbook of her own life; it also gave her pieces of her grandmother's.

Dear God,

Help me to practice theology

according to my grandmother's quilt:

Life is always made

of contrasts and nothing need be wasted,

not even time.

Amen.

THE GRADUATION QUILT

Do not despise this small beginning,
for the eyes of the Lord rejoice to see the work begin.

ZECHARIAH 4:10 TLB

She wanted to graduate from high school. Sometimes, her mother thought, she seemed to want it more than a boyfriend or a clear complexion. It was the goal that pushed her to move painful arthritic joints from classroom to classroom. It drove her to spend the extra hours it took to study for a test or dictate an essay. Even special education resources weren't "special" enough to make up for the gaps in her brain. Like retrieving a childhood memory buried by years of other experiences, yesterday's information remained entombed, and there was no one to roll the stone away.

"Mom, do you think I will ever graduate?" Lisa queried, contemplating the hours and books and classes looming ahead of her like an unforgiving Everest.

"I don't know," her mother always answered truthfully. "All we can do is finish this semester and see what comes next."

There were times Lisa's mother thought she should quit. She had no leisure time. There were no easy subjects. And there was no one who faced the same combined mental, physical, and social challenges. Together, they drilled, reworded, color coded, and charted everything for easy retrieval. If only they could do the same inside the tangled and short-circuited network they knew her brain to be.

That's why the closer they got to graduation, the more plans they made to celebrate. No small party for this achievement. Pull out all the stops. Finally, it was time to praise Lisa's victory. Family and friends asked her mother for gift ideas. They wanted to match the gift to the accomplishment. But how do you fitly memorialize a climb that has taken twenty-one years to make?

It was then that Lisa's grandmother announced she was making her a graduation quilt. Both mother and daughter began to realize how many people had watched helplessly as Lisa made her torturous uphill climb. They were ready for victory too.

As Lisa's grandmother brought the first squares for her mother's approval, the message quilted into the masterpiece emerged. Each square was a lace-lined heart.

Hadn't it taken a lot of heart for Lisa to be left out of life in her pursuit of a dream? Hadn't it taken a lot of heart to sit with her note-taker at the back of the room, while many of her classmates labeled her dumb and a misfit? Hadn't it taken a lot of heart to walk through the school halls with her robotic gait, despite the teasing and put-downs? Hadn't it taken a lot of heart to meet the stares of each new class and work with teachers who tried to understand her learning gaps but never really did?

There they were—heart after heart, one for each struggle and covered with lace. Wasn't that what God had promised? Not to change the struggle but to create something beautiful from it?

After Lisa went to bed at night or while she was at school, her mother watched as her grandmother inserted tiny stitches, thousands of them. One after another, she bobbed her needle in and out, painstakingly covering the quilt with hearts made of her stitches.

There was so much truth in those tiny stitches. It didn't matter how tiny they were. One step, or stitch, after another always takes you farther. It took Lisa all the way to graduation. Now, her mother wondered where the steps would take her next.

She thought of all the meetings, all the study hours, all the phone calls it took to make graduation a reality for this undaunted dreamer. She thought of the unfairness, the inequity, the frustration, the tears. But for now the struggle had given way to accomplishment, the pain to summit victory. In her black robe and tasseled cap, there was a final justice in the sameness.

The quilt commanded center stage among Lisa's many lovely gifts. A work of the heart, it celebrated her stubborn determination in the face of brick walls and closed doors. It will always say "graduation." It will always mean hope. Today it rests, protected, inside a closet for the day it will decorate a wall, a stand, or a bed in her own home. That's the new dream. And it will take many, many more stitches.

Dear God,

Forgive my complaints for tiny steps and repetitive pathways. Help me understand the worth of a dream and the value of the climb. Remind me often that the finished work, like the finished quilt, does not show the struggle with knotted tangles along the way. When I celebrate the victory, I also embrace the process. Amen.

— — — —

THE DOLL QUILT

We will tell the next generation.

PSALM 78:4

Victoria was her favorite doll. Her delicately chiseled features resembled a real baby. Her stitched, stuffed but unjointed arms and legs fell as helpless as a newborn in the arms of a little mother. Easy to cuddle, fun to dress, Victoria held her own against Cabbage Patch and Cut-and-Grow and all the other additions to Sara's doll nursery.

But the porcelain doll her aunt made was different. Dressed in a long white christening gown, bonneted with lace and ribbon, this doll was as fragile as Victoria only looked. Sara's parents cautioned her to be careful with her new charge. This doll was not to be played with. She was just for show.

But Sara couldn't resist giving her a few buggy rides around the house, and one day, the inevitable happened. While taking the fragile china doll out of the buggy, Sara dropped her. It was difficult to know who was more broken. The doll with three pieces of her cranium on the floor or Sara's heart? Sara's dad-turned-neurosurgeon carefully glued her dolly's head together, but permanent scars still show beneath the carefully placed bonnet.

That was the china doll's last buggy ride. After the fall, Sara agreed to put her away until she could be displayed in a stay-in-one-place way.

It was a move and a larger room that brought the china doll out of the box. The doll nursery was moved to a basement playroom complete with doll beds, high chair, buggy, and play kitchen. That left space in Sara's bedroom for the china doll to rest securely in a basket crib where her fragile beauty could be shared by all. Soon after, Sara's grandfather made a rocking cradle for the china doll, and not to be outdone, her grandmother made a mattress, pillow, and doll quilt.

The doll quilt was on show as much as the china doll or cradle. Its yellow and pink pieces declared childhood in every square. The "Basket" square held diamond flowers like the childhood bouquets Sara loved to collect, and the quilted figures of a bunny, an elephant, and a little girl finished out the six-square creation. How easily childhood embraces such contrasts.

The doll quilt connected Sara's mother to her own childhood and the doll crib and quilt made for her by her grandmother, her mother's mother. The quilt was pieced from mattress ticking left over from her aunt's home-based sewing business. Doll-sized but so very real looking, her doll quilt had covered her dolls, had become a pallet for them on the floor, and occasionally had been rolled into a pillow for her own head.

She hadn't given much thought to her doll quilt until Sara received hers. Then, she realized how generations repeat themselves by more than genes. The quilting tradition in her family was not blood-locked. It had truly been handed down—the art of handwork. At the end of a day of laundry and dishes and office work, Sara's mother learned from her mother how to work with her hands. She learned that the gift of doll-sized replications was more valuable than Barbie clothes or a new stuffed animal. None of her friends could boast of a homemade doll quilt to perfectly fit a doll bed. Her doll quilt had value in its single existence.

It is a grandmother's prerogative to give what a mother does not have time or money to give. And one day when Sara's mother no longer has to meet schedules and race to finish household chores, she will find a grandmother's time to pass on simple treasures to her own granddaughter. Even though her gift may not be quilting, she will find some other handwork to pass on, and the generational circle will continue.

Dear God,

May I pass on the simple treasures
that cannot be mass-produced.
May I accept the generational circle
that demands a time and priority change
that will perpetuate the circle.
May I learn the value of a doll quilt
even after it no longer covers a doll.
Amen.

THE PALLET

Greater love has no one than this,
that he lay down his life for his friends.

JOHN 15:13

"I t's time for your nap."

Phoebe's five-year-old body revolted. Her face melted into a grimace. Her voice pitched its whine. Her right foot stomped rebellion.

"I don't want to take a nap!"

Why she thought her wants mattered in this naptime routine was uncertain. Perhaps she understood her defenseless position and used it as a last stand before the surrender she knew would always come.

"I'll make you a pallet on the floor in your room," her mother negotiated.

Suddenly she took to the pallet idea as if it had no connection to nap. She dropped her toys in the same way she dropped her whine.

"On the pink quilt?" she asked, swept into the magic of getting her own way.

"On the pink quilt," her mother affirmed.

And so it was that the pink quilt her grandmother had made became Phoebe's naptime pallet. What started out as compromise became routine. For some reason, naptime on the floor was not the same as naptime on her bed. She laid her head on the colored pieces and explored the terrain with her fingers. Her grandmother's gingham was set prominently in several squares, and Phoebe seemed to lie as peacefully on those gingham strips as she did in her grandmother's lap—the lap that held crochet thread, beans to string, corn to shuck, and often Phoebe herself.

Phoebe and her grandmother had lived in the same house as long as she could remember. For her, it meant that there was always a free lap to lie in. Even when Mother and Father were busy, Grandmother was always a welcomed substitute. Phoebe had watched her grandmother stitch the quilt from remnants of clothing she had sewn for others in the family circle—her big sister's short set, her mother's shirtwaist dress, Easter clothes, aprons, and doll clothes. All these items surrounded her on this pallet like they surrounded her in life. To place her head anywhere on the pallet was to touch the people of her small world.

For a couple of hours in the middle of the day, Phoebe's world became the quilt. Her fingers walked the stitched pathways—Polka Dot Avenue, Gingham Corner, Taffeta Circle. She loved to lie at different corners as if to change her scenery. Soon the isolation and the pallet worked its magic. While focusing on a flurry of flowers, her eyelids would soon droop and close. She slept, without the staccato sniff of a child put to bed in tears. She slept in the lap of her grandmother on a pieced garden of throwaway scraps.

Everybody needs a grandmother's lap. Perhaps that's why Phoebe still uses this quilt, not for a bed, but for a pallet. She has rested visiting babies on this quilt and laid it out for her own daughter's nap, trusting it to work the same magic. The quilt never quite had the same effect on others though. Phoebe could see that the real magic of the quilt was not the cotton print or stitched together pieces. It was rooted in the love between a grandmother and a granddaughter. It was triggered by the delight she had found in her grandmother's lap—a place where she often rested, listened to stories, shelled peas, played dolls, and fell peacefully to sleep. To Phoebe the quilt was magical because it represented a grandmother's love.

From time to time, Phoebe still lays the pink-blocked pallet on the floor and lies down to nap. Even now, these many years after her grandmother's death, Phoebe still feels as if she is lying in her lap. She walks its treasured pieces with her fingers, and she vows to make her own lap and her life a quiet and secure place for others to rest, play, cry, or laugh. She promises to take the altered realities of those who are hurting and treat them as seriously as her grandmother treated her doll games. She knows better than to change her reality to fit theirs, but perhaps in the course of letting the game run out, she will be able to help someone put away their childish perspective and find security in facing the truth.

Did her grandmother's lap teach her all that? Perhaps not, but it did prepare Phoebe to learn it. And the pallet quilt still holds its magic for her—not for naptime but for life. To make her life a pallet, she must first lay it down.

— — — —

Dear God,

Make my life a pallet for someone's wearied walk.
Let my heart be listening when someone needs to talk.
Piece my love together, use Your wisdom in each square.
Help me show the lonely that You are always there.

Let me nudge the heartsick to stop and take a nap.
Instead of pallet sleeping, let me show them to Your lap.
For in Your lap they'll find a rest like nothing sleep can give.
No longer will they fear Your will, no longer fugitive.

Let them linger long and still until the sleep has passed,
Until the strengthened napper finds a courage that will last.
And when they wake renewed and strong,
I'll take my pallet-life
To lay before another who needs to heal from life.
Amen.

CHARLCIE'S QUILTS

Accept one another, then, just as Christ accepted you.

They are garish, without artistic pattern. Wools and jersey, geometrics and polka dots war against a few subtle prints. Rectangular blocks, not even uniform in size, lie like bricks on this fortress wall of unmatched color. The red zigzag stitches add nothing to this mix of too modern and very outdated. Backed with the pink percale of a secondhand sheet, this quilt is a living testimony to the adage: *Waste not, want not.* There is no waste here. Everything but the thread and machine is secondhand.

Debbie has four of these quilts that will never appear in anyone's quilt show. She doesn't even use them on the beds in her house. They are stored in the garage for impromptu picnics. They have covered furniture for moving or storage. They are nothing if not sturdy. Debbie thinks they might be made to last for eternity.

Debbie stores Charlcie's quilts in the garage, but she keeps the memories of her friend very close, as close as family—especially their first meeting.

Charlcie lived across the street from the first church Debbie's husband, Mark, pastored. She became surrogate grandmother to Lisa when Mark's first wife died of cancer. When Debbie married Mark and became Lisa's new mother, she was not prepared for the power struggle that awaited.

Debbie sat in the lawn chair on a pleasant Texas afternoon, waiting to meet this woman who was already a legend in her new family. But she heard her gravelly voice before she ever saw her face. Charlcie came up behind her and put her hands over Debbie's eyes to "surprise" her. The wiry woman with no style to her hair or clothing owned a flair as unique as her name. Wearing pedal pushers and an unmatched short-sleeved blouse, she was as out of style as the rest of her house.

Charlcie and her husband Nathan lived like hermits in a house with closed blinds to keep out more than the sun. They raised chickens in the backyard and used the car only when absolutely necessary. They bought food begrudgingly from the grocery store and only what they could not raise themselves. Charlcie and Nathan sat in their matching recliners watching game shows all day long, except when they read *Reader's Digest* or the newspaper. They were relics from a different time and created as many wrinkles in Debbie's life as they both wore on their faces.

They had "adopted" Lisa before she was born. Childless, they looked forward to this new baby on their block with as much enthusiasm as a blood relative. One of the first visitors to the hospital, Charlcie tentatively asked for baby-sitting privileges, much to the surprise of the infant's two very new parents.

It was during Lisa's six months of colic that Charlcie endeared herself. She could hear the exhausted cries of this newborn whether she was in her crib at home or across the street at church. More times than anyone can count, she rescued the screaming baby from frustrated arms and walked her with more patience than she gave to anyone else in her world.

When Debbie came into the picture, she challenged the comfortable circle Charlcie had made for herself and Lisa. She was the only daycare Lisa had ever known outside her own home and family. Charlcie had accustomed herself to extensive time with Lisa during the week and on the weekend as well. And then along came Debbie, a stranger with claims that overrode her own. To make matters worse, Lisa preferred her time with Charlcie (her Ma-maw), who gave her anything she wanted—from ice cream to popsicles and let her wear anything anywhere.

Debbie learned to tolerate Charlcie's Friday-Saturday claims to Lisa. She also learned to put the child in the bathtub as soon as she returned from Charlcie's house. While these two women never exactly "shared" Lisa, they each came to appreciate the place the other had in her life.

More important was the place Lisa had in Charlcie's and Nathan's lives. She was literally the light in their darkness. Lisa made them say grace before eating. Lisa made them hide their cigarettes and alcohol. There was nothing they wouldn't do for "that baby."

Charlcie's quilts were part of her charity work. She collected bags of remnants, cut, pieced, and machine quilted them while locked inside her air-conditioned house in the heat of Texas summers. Who knows how many quilts she gave away. Debbie has only four.

A quilt is a good memorial to Charlcie, this woman whose life-pieces didn't seem to fit. The contrasts were as numerous as pieces of any of her quilts. She lived like a pauper but had enough money from land investments to secure an above average financial standing. She rarely attended the church but would have fought anyone who challenged the placement of her name in the church directory. She voiced an opinion about everything, especially about things she feared or did not understand. She was fiercely loyal and outrageously prejudiced. Charlcie herself was a quilt of many pieces—sturdy, created to last, but not for show.

Debbie would tell you that Charlcie taught her many things about herself. How her insecurity hid behind what she claimed were a mother's rights. How she was more comfortable sharing her world with Charlcie and bristled when the tables were turned. How she did not know what to do with someone who found the ability to love almost too late but only knew how to focus it one way. How she was not as flexible or tolerant as she had always thought.

Charlcie taught Debbie honesty in the pieces of her quilt. She made no claims except that she made them to keep people warm. And when Debbie went to her house already practicing the reasons Lisa could not stay another night, was she as honest? The truth was that they both loved Lisa but demonstrated it in different ways.

Even now, when Debbie reflects on those Texas memories with her quilt of many colors in front of her, she feels the struggle inside. Charlcie had taught her how to make a place for a wildly quilted life in her world of gentle colors and artistic patterns.

Today, all Debbie has left of Charlcie are her quilts, her pictures, and the memory of her gravelly voice and lung-rattling cough. But there is a new place in her heart and life for a square unlike all the other squares in her quilt of many patterns. It is the Charlcie square with all its garish color and differences. It teaches her even now that she has nothing to share with another person when her inner self pushes its needs to the forefront. It teaches her that learning to let God meet or redefine her need is part of putting away childish things. She wishes she had learned the lessons before she met Charlcie. Their relationship might have been marked less by need and more by love.

Maybe it's time to bring the Charlcie quilts out of

the garage. Or maybe Debbie just needs to live their lesson with all the other Charlcies in her world.

Dear God,

I am sometimes all need,

and You are always all-sufficient.

When I apply Your sufficiency to my need,

I am ready to see another's need, to love more

than tolerate, to accept more than judge.

Amen.

PART III

PARABLES

Quilts, like parables, tell stories that teach.

MOTHER'S QUILT

Who is my mother?

MATTHEW 12:48

I t was something she always wanted to do: make a
quilt. Her mother and her mother's mother had
always made them. In her family, it was kind of a rite
of passage into womanhood.

Yet Susan was surprised when her mother signed up
for a beginner's quilting class. Unlike the age-old tradition of using scraps and collected pieces, she bought her
fabric new. It was Williamsburg blue and eggshell ivory.
She marked the material and cut the pieces.

She worked on it off and on for a year. It was just a
hobby that had no deadline, perfect for snatches of
unscheduled time, which were few for this busy working
woman. She would finish in the kitchen, gather her
quilting bag, and take a seat in the living room, while the
rest of the family settled into their own worlds of
end-of-the-day study or TV.

In the beginning, quilting took her full focus. New
skills always do. She found a peace in the quiet world

of silent stitches that the rest of her world did not give her. More and more, she picked up the bag and the orderly world it made out of the pieces of her own. But still, the end of the project seemed years away.

Susan and her mother talked about quilting off and on. She had never known her mother to have a hobby, so busy was she with necessary chores. So this was new—something that didn't have to be done, something she chose and liked, something that liked her back.

One day in their mother-daughter exchange, Susan's mother shared a secret joy. "The instructor was impressed with my stitches," she declared like a schoolgirl who just brought home an "A" on her class work. Her statement stunned Susan, who had always thought that her mother could do anything and everything. This twinge of awkward modesty seemed an incongruity. It was as though her mother had become a woman just like herself, full of awkward insecurities and wearing a schoolgirl smile.

Perhaps that is why it meant so much when Susan unfolded the still unfinished quilt the night before her wedding. It was more than a gift; it represented her mother's new identity. She had found a new security and a new confidence with each stitch. Or rather it found her.

Her first quilt. *Nothing is quite as exceptional as first works,* Susan thought. The fact that her mother had given her this wonderful gift would bind them together as women, both on a journey of self-discovery, both continuing to run to each other when the journey became harsh or painful.

The quilt took nearly a year to finish. Susan had passed from honeymoon to the honeyed life of newly married by the time her mother packed the finished quilt in her suitcase and came for a visit. It was an exquisite piece of work. Her nearly microscopic stitches in fine, straight lines looked almost machine-produced. But no machine could quilt its design with the signature of this quilter.

Susan thought this would be her mother's last quilt. It wasn't. She started one for Susan's sister, added one for their brother, completed one for each grandchild, and finally found time to make one for herself.

But Susan delighted in the fact that hers was the first—an inauguration of her mother's confidence and skill, a mirror into her soul, a gift of time for time to come.

Today, her mother's quilt rests on Susan's guest room bed to protect it from overuse. One day, perhaps it will have to be stored. However, it will always remind her of the time when she understood her mother as a woman and herself as her peer, forever connected by womanhood and not just by blood.

O God,

In the same umbilical way that the quilt connected us
as women, may the rest of our days connect us as friends.
May we share the circle of life and love,
which forgets its place of beginning and knows no end.
Amen.

UNDERCOVER

He will cover you.

PSALM 91:4

Growing up in Kansas City winters, she often slept in a two-quilt bed. Quilts provide more weight and insulation than blankets. While snuggled underneath, she believed that the quilt coverings kept out the cold. Really, it kept her body heat in. Whatever the thermodynamics, when the temperature dipped to single digits and below, Sharon wanted to be warm.

Unless she and her sister sat up to watch the late movie, Sharon usually went to bed while the house was still warm. Part of her dad's evening ritual was to lower the thermostat before retiring into the cold dark of night. That meant that often she would start off with one quilt and then, sometime during the night or early morning, add the second. She would pull it to her ears, enjoy the illusion that weight adds warmth, and sleep, cocooned, for the rest of the night.

Sharon especially remembers waking up under two quilts on Saturday mornings. She was not an early riser and loved to lie underneath the weight of her two quilts and read. She would arrange the quilt to tent her in warmth, covering as much flesh as possible. She would then allow only her page-turning hand to peek outside the covers while every other part of her body stayed toasty warm. Before frostbite set in, she would switch sides to warm the cold hand and wake up the sleeping arm. It is an imprinted pattern she still uses when reading in bed.

Sharon came to like the weight of the quilts whether they vacuum-sealed her for the night or insulated her against the cold of a new-morning house. To her way of thinking, they gave more than warmth. They gave security. They held her in place and hugged her during the night. They made it difficult for her to leave their hold the next morning in a furnace-heated house not yet warmed for the day. Perhaps that is why she's still not an early riser. She blames it on the quilts.

Today, it takes more than a two-quilt bed to give her the security she needs. And the warmth that sustains her is not under the covers. Today, Sharon has grown past her Saturday-morning cocoon. Usually her day's agenda cannot be finished if she spends the morning snuggled in the bedding.

— — — —

But Sharon still sleeps in a two-quilt bed when she returns for Christmas to the Midwestern town of her adolescence. She sinks beneath the covers with only her head bobbing outside. Like a deep-heat treatment, she soaks in this quilt-made sauna and rests under this impenetrable armor against everything cold. Safe. Secure. It makes her feel like a child again in her mother's house.

Sharon sleeps under a blanket at home. The quilts are too heavy. And when morning comes, she gets out of bed . . . after the cup of coffee her husband brings her. But she is grateful for the lessons she learned from her two-quilt bed.

She learned how God covers her with Himself in a way that prevents the need for anything artificial. And that no matter how good and warm and secure something feels, the real test of security is what it makes you do. God's security always encourages her to choose wisely, speak kindly, love unconditionally, and live obediently.

Sharon will always enjoy the two-quilt bed of her youth. But she knows now that when it comes to security for life, God is the best covering.

O God,

Will You cover me like a quilt?

In every night, through every cold

and lonely place, wherever fear threatens,

snuggle close and cover me.

Be my daily reminder to an everlasting source of

comfort, grace, and strength.

Be my spiritual hiding place

for rest or healing.

At the close of a day or in the middle

of rejection or isolation, will You comfort, quilt,

and cover me with Your love?

Amen.

AT MIZ HILLEY'S

She [gave] out of her poverty.
MARK 12:44

"I t's a long road that never turns."

She rolled her words, rounded their edges, and slipped them between lips that no longer hid teeth.

"But it gets kinda crooked."

Her small head bobbed from the pillow as she punched her words with ninety-plus years of experience. Miss Fredna Hilley lay in the nursing home bed in a pastel green, lace-edged gown. Her friends and family knew it would be her last home, and there was great sadness as well as comfort in that truth.

It must have been a good day because she recognized the three boys, now grown men, who had sat around her fireplace, slept under her quilts, eaten her biscuits, and grown up within the circle of her love.

"Miz" Hilley, as the boys called her, never married. She lived with her two brothers, Morris and Wayne. That was a generation behind the age of indoor plumbing and electricity. That's why the boys enjoyed going to

Miz Hilley's house. It was a place not at all like home.

For many years there was no electricity. Oil lamps and a bedroom fireplace were the only sources of evening light. When the boys were young and their mother and father made one of their infrequent out-of-town trips, they stayed with Miz Hilley, where they were tucked snuggly under warm quilts in the winter.

The house where Miz Hilley lived had a boulder holding up the back porch, and you could see the ground through the floor slats. It had only two warm places. One was in front of the fireplace, where Miz Hilley, with great expression and conviction, read the Bible to the boys. No one had to tell them to be quiet when Miz Hilley read. Her eyes would grow as big as silver dollars and her face would bear the likeness to each character of whom she read. As fire shadows licked the walls, the boys would sit hypnotized by each biblical rebuke or loving encounter. And they grew warm within the reach of her voice and her fire.

But there was another warm place in the Hilley house. It was in the bed under many quilts. Miz Hilley kept a quilt frame in one of the rooms. In a home that had few sources of heat, quilts were not for show; they were for warmth. Before the boys bedded down, Miz Hilley would place a brick on the wood cookstove. When it was good and hot, she would wrap it in towels and put it in the bed at just the right place for little boys' feet. Nothing ever felt so warm as lying in Miz Hilley's brick-warmed bed under a pile of homemade quilts.

"Do you remember when we used to come to your house?" one of the boys asked.

"Uh-huh!" She punctuated each syllable with more energy than it seemed her frail form had to give. "I still love every one of you."

She could squeeze the boys in a bear hug with her penetrating eyes. Flash and fire spoke a resilience in great contrast to her physical weakness. She had been a strong woman. It was her character. Aging took away her plump form, her coordination, and the calcium from her bones. But it could not rob her of her character. Strong as Georgia pine she was, even bedridden.

Miz Hilley was born and raised in Stark, Georgia.

"Lots worse things than living in Stark." She did not just speak. She gathered her words from longtime memories, squeezed them into a simple package, and tossed them as if playing catch.

Stark, Georgia, isn't much more than an intersection and a few buildings today. What it must have been when she grew up there, the boys could not imagine, but the name appropriately communicated the plain and simple life Miz Hilley must have lived there.

At the Hilley house, the boys sat in the laps of two brothers, Morris and Wayne, who knew nothing about fathering but everything about little boys. With more patience than any father, they taught the boys to drive mules with the traditional commands "gee" and "ha." They taught them that you *chop* cotton; you don't hoe it. They tried to teach them to milk cows, but either the cows or the boys were slow learners. The Hilley brothers never needed to know which.

And the Hilley brothers would always make ice cream for the boys in the summer. They would buy ice from town, a small extravagance. But the rest of the ingredients came from their farm—fresh cream, butter, and eggs still warm from the nest. Ice cream in the wooden hand-turned maker was better than anything you could get at a store or a stand.

"The Lord works in mysterious ways. Don't underestimate the ways of the Lord," Miz Hilley would say. It was a sermon in two sentences, and it summarized her statement of faith. The Lord works—a testimony and a truth. This frail and feeble witness was still testifying to the unapproachable understanding of God's ways while she lay attached to oxygen. She spoke with pioneer confidence. She had made enough of the journey so that nothing that lay in her future could make her doubt this truth. While context reduced her life baggage, it only made her more ready for her eternal destination.

A blue blanket warmed her slight body and covered her knobby knees that made dual hills under the covers. She would not be here long, and the boys squeezed every memory and truth from those moments.

"I've got a good appetite, and sometimes I forget about it," Miz Hilley said, throwing in another bundle of words that the boys caught, laughing. She searched each face as if memorizing features or retrieving some lost image or thought.

"Well, well, well," she whispered, punctuating the room with her eyes. They were wide and bright as tin pie pans hanging in tomato gardens to catch the Georgia sun. She had worked many a garden, hoed many a row. The boys had eaten her tomatoes and other produce as a treat, not realizing the poverty from which they came.

Are you poor if you don't know it? Or is poverty more perception than fact? The boys now understand how little the Hilleys had. They also understand that being poor is more than just having little. The Hilleys always had enough to share. They shared their fire, their biscuits, their mules, their ice cream, their quilts, and their hearts.

The boys circled this woman from their youth, took turns patting her hand, and said their good-byes. When they left the room where Miz Hilley lay, they walked out with fresh memories and a new definition of wealth. No one would ever call Miz Hilley wealthy. But these boys-become-men would fight anyone who ever called her poor. No one is poor who has that much to give.

O God,

Why is it that I think I must always have more in order to give? True poverty has less to do with what you have and more to do with what you won't share. I want to be rich by Your definition. I want to be known more by what I share than by what I keep. Will You help me?

Amen.

— — — —

THE GOOD-BYE QUILT

Do not dwell on the past.

ISAIAH 43:18

It was time to go. The boxes and bare walls confirmed the fact. Jane's hands were paper-dry with generous newsprint smudges. It was a challenge to put a whole house inside boxes. It was more of a challenge to do it neatly in case a prospective buyer wanted to see the house.

Jane and her family had made their rounds of all their favorite St. Louis spots. In lieu of photographs, they had catalogued ten years of memories by heart. There had been ten years of birthdays and anniversaries here. They had purchased their first home here. They had made a lot of friends over barbecues and Sunday dinners. The heart bonds went deep. While friends cannot be boxed and moved, friendship would make many invisible journeys with them.

Their friends threw a good-bye party for them. They teased Jane's husband about his Georgia drawl, and they affirmed the many bridges they had crossed together, marking births, deaths, weddings, and other special times. They gave them gifts. Jane loved the gold-lipped crystal goblets and looked forward to using them on every special occasion. But the gift that meant the most, the gift that now hangs in the family room of their new home, is the good-bye quilt.

The quilter was new to their church family. She had won the sack of quilt scraps from a drawing at her quilters' group. It was a haphazard assortment of dated and contemporary, paisley and print. She used a square pattern that opened in a kaleidoscope of squares within squares. Church members wrote their names on some of the three-by-three-inch squares. Children added their scribbles. Each left an indelible imprint on the quilt and on the lives of the receivers.

There was the new Christian who had made an 180-degree turn in her life. The Italian butcher who learned to forgive his father before his father's death closed the door forever. The couple whose third and fourth children died by miscarriage and stillbirth and the woman who crushed her face but not her spirit in a car accident. Each square with a name was a square with a story.

Jane still remembers unpacking the good-bye quilt

in her new home. She used it to fight the Northwest chill that caused her Midwest frame to shiver and to wrap herself with familiar arms as she adjusted to her new environment.

The good-bye quilt helped Jane say good-bye in the right way. It told her she had closed a chapter in her life. It reminded her that she had started a new one and provided a tangible bridge between the two.

Jane has kept up with most of the people represented by the squares in her good-bye quilt. She still hears about the births, weddings, and funerals back in Saint Louis. She knows that they will never be together again with those particular friends, at least not in the way the quilt had patterned them. But they will always be quilted together somewhere in their hearts. For nothing, not even good-bye, changes what was. And only clinging to what was and will never be again can skew the future.

Now, when Jane wraps herself in the good-bye quilt, she realizes that she does not wrap herself in the past, for the *good* in good-bye is for tomorrow.

Dear God,

I cringe at good-byes. I fear them,

postpone them,

and sometimes refuse to deal with them.

Help me see how I tie Your hands

when I bind myself to the past.

Gather all the good in every good-bye

and teach me how to use it

to welcome tomorrow.

Amen.

THE OLD CHURCH QUILT

Consider the generations long past.

DEUTERONOMY 32:7

As soon as she unfolded it, Diane knew there was a story. Embroidered in each square was a name, sometimes a date, and often a verse. Though age had frayed the edges and pulled some threads, most of the names remained legible.

It read like a church attendance record. Diane had learned its history. In 1936, thirty women had signed their names and acknowledged their bond. That was a difficult year for many of the families named. Work was scarce. But hard times either push people apart or bring them together, and Diane could see that these people quilted themselves together in an ever-enlarging circle.

It was the work of the women of the Missionary Society of the church. They worked from quilt frames in the basement. The women met to hear about missions, pray for missions, and plan church projects for missions. Since "idle hands are the devil's tools," the women kept their hands busy with quilting.

For a time, the quilt covered Grandma Henry's bed with love and memories. Grandma Henry was a charter member of the church that made the quilt. When Grandma Henry died, the quilt went to her daughter, Birdie, with other artifacts uncovered when her house was emptied.

Birdie became a second-generation circle for the quilt and the church. When Birdie died, the quilt went to her son and daughter-in-law in the tradition of passing on possessions to the next of kin.

It was here that the quilt circle was almost broken. While they kept the quilt, they did not step inside its circle. The quilt became a family heirloom only. They stored it like their picture albums and seldom brought it out. It did not connect them to the circle of the church. It shared no stories of the people who sewed their names into squares. It kindled no memories, except of their mother and mother-in-law. And even then, the stories of the quilt were silent because its language was locked in relationships this new generation did not share.

However, when asked, they shared their mother's church story—how a group of women quilted the squares, embroidered beauty, and left their legacy to a church and each other in every stitch. They told their mother and grandmother valued the quilt, not as a work of art but as a work of the heart.

But that's not the end of the story. When Birdie's son had surgery, the family found the circle where the quilt began. The surgeon and his wife, a nurse, belonged to the same church the quilt had come from. Conversation traced the family back to its 1936 church involvement. To thank this physician and wife for their skill and compassion, Birdie's family presented them with the old church quilt.

The quilt had come full circle, invisibly adding family names and experiences. Daughters of these early quilters are now, themselves, seniors. At the sight of the names on this old church quilt, stories and faces and another time live again. It is again a history of a church and shares the truth that a circle grows by enlarging its reach.

Just as the circle of this quilt reached past the circle of its origin, our lives will do the same. And what we pass on will have value as it enables others to draw a circle that reaches past our earth-quilted lives all the way to God.

Most of the original quilters are now gone. But

three things they worked on remain: their families, their church, and this quilt.

There are new quilters in the basement of the church today. They make their quilts and work on their circles of life. They share their stories and stitch themselves together. Each quilt begins a new circle, stitched one day at a time.

Dear God,

*What part of life is legacy and what part has
little lasting value? Sometimes I have difficulty
telling the difference. Too often I save the wrong things
to give away. Remind me that legacy lives more in priorities
than possessions. Warn me against waiting too long
to live my legacy. Help me start today.*

Amen.

MAKE MY LIFE
A CIRCLE, GOD

Make my life a circle, God
For I do not know the stitches.
Let me leave my life as a legacy
Sharing value that enriches.

May I understand that circle
Quilts a story line by line.
May I find the way to leave mine
In a quilting bold and fine.

But always hold before me
That the circle I am in
Was a circle gone before me
And a circle with no end.

Help me trace Your patterned stitches
In the circle that You lived.
Reaching all the way to Heaven
With the life You came to give.

Make my life a circle, God,
With a long elastic reach.
Make me know each day my stitches
Are values I will teach.

Make it rich with acts of meaning
Lessons pure by heart turned new;
Making generation bridges
Reaching all the way to You.

A SECURITY QUILT

You are my security.

JOB 31:24

Teresa was home from college for Christmas break. The holiday gave her everything she didn't have at college: home-cooked meals, leisure, privacy, and family.

It was evening, that golden time after the dishes were chuggling in the dishwasher and quiet drew its curtain between family and everything else. They were reading, mother and daughter, enjoying that strange companionship that draws people together in silence.

Anna broke the silence with a request, asking her daughter for the quilt from the corner. Teresa reached for it but stopped in discovery's paralysis. Threads of unraveling cloth testified that this was the quilt she used to sleep with, twisted around her body with a corner in her mouth. And not just any corner. Always the same one.

Touching the corner took her back to the time when they had gone to Aunt Lilly's house. She remembered crying the whole night because no one thought to pack the quilt. The quilt didn't just give warmth, it gave

---

security. It hid her from the dark when her mother wasn't there to push it away.

When was it that I stopped sleeping with the quilt? Teresa wondered. It had been on her bed as long as she could remember. But somewhere along the line, she had learned that leaving home didn't mean leaving security. It meant finding new sources for it. It meant learning to depend on God.

Teresa took the quilt of many lessons and covered her mother. As she did, she understood how much they both needed security blankets. Is that why her mother kept the quilt in the corner? For her own brand of insecurity attacks?

She returned to her book, determined to sleep with the quilt again—not because she needed the warmth or the security but because she treasured its lessons.

Dear God,

Security is a scarce commodity in our society. We lean on such useless crutches to find some sense of stability. And there You are, the God from always was to always will be, permanent and changeless, magnificently available. Save me from pointless searches for security that can only be found in You. Amen.

— — — —

A TIDING OF COMFORT

*How beautiful . . . are the feet of those . . .
who bring good news.*

ISAIAH 52:7

"How's Grandma?" seven-year-old Karin asked after plopping school books on the counter.

"There's no change," her mother answered, turning away to hide the worry she could not put into words.

It had started with a cold. Then they took her to the hospital. Pneumonia. When Karin's parents explained it to her, her mother had told her that grandmother's illness made it difficult and painful for her to breathe.

Karin took a deep breath and let it out slowly. If it hurt to breathe, maybe you wouldn't try to do it so much, she reasoned. So she tried making each breath last longer. But the urge to take in air was too great. Before she knew it, she had gulped a mouthful.

Thinking about her grandmother lying in a hospital taking painful breaths seemed to take away all Karin's Christmas cheer. What would Christmas be without Grandmother's cookies and stories and her Adventcalendar treats? She pushed the more difficult questions to the back of her mind and asked her mother, "Will Grandmother be home for Christmas?"

"We hope so, dear," her mother answered.

Short answers did not seem like a good sign. Karin took her fear and her mother's expression away to her bedroom. She threw herself down on the bed and put her head on the quilt folded at the foot. The texture of the stitched patterns diverted her attention. Swirls and swirls of tiny stitches covered the quilt like an ant trail from scattered crumbs. Her grandmother had made the quilt. She had made each one of her grandchildren a quilt. It rested, folded at the foot of the bed, to add warmth and comfort to her cold nights. Now, the maker of the quilt hurt when she breathed.

In the days that followed, Karin could think of little else than her grandmother's painful breathing. As young minds reinvent the literal world, Karin came to believe that if she could do something to take away the pain, she would be able to bring her grandmother home. It wasn't enough that doctors and nurses were helping. Somehow Karin believed she had to help. But how?

The idea came to her at church. Like the first star

of the night, it broke through her darkness. The choir had sung it and the pastor had preached it—tidings of comfort—tidings to chase away pain—tidings to turn back sadness.

That was what her grandmother needed: a tiding to take away her pain, a tiding to make her comfortable, a tiding to bring her home for Christmas. She would send her grandmother a tiding of comfort.

She was so full of her new idea that it didn't occur to her that she didn't know how to send a tiding. She didn't even know what a tiding was. She only knew that her grandmother needed one.

She asked her father first.

"Dad, what's a tiding?"

"Well, it's . . . a . . . message."

"Like our Christmas cards?"

"Yes, something like that."

And before her father could add to his answer, Karin began hatching the next part of her plan. She would send her tiding just like she mailed a Christmas card.

She ran to her room awash with a mission. But then

she stopped. What tiding of comfort would she send? She looked around her room and saw the quilt that had often comforted her. It was perfect. She would send her the quilt.

Karin went to the basement and found a box. Then she rolled the quilt into a bundle as tightly as she could and stuffed it into the box. She took her favorite kitten stationery and wrote her grandmother an explanation.

Grandma,

When it hurts to breathe, here is a tiding of comfort.

Love,

Karin.

She taped the box shut, emptying a roll of clear sticky tape. Then, she wrote her grandmother's name on the box. Now to mail it. It was the next day that she walked into the post office with her package in her arms, waited her turn, and pushed the box onto the counter.

"Please, sir, I'd like to mail this tiding of comfort to my grandmother at the hospital."

"Well, now, I've mailed Christmas cards and packages, even sent letters to Santa Claus at the North Pole, but I don't think I've ever mailed a tiding. Are you some kind of angel or something?" the mail clerk asked.

"I don't think so. It's just that my grandmother is sick in the hospital and needs a tiding of comfort."

The mail clerk stopped mid-laugh, for he saw in Karin's eyes the reason behind every card and package he'd ever stamped and posted for delivery. He decided that this young Christmas angel might need some help to complete her mission, and he would give it.

"I think all of us could use that kind of tiding. Let's see how we can get this one on its way." With that, he weighed the box, completed the address, told her the cost, and helped her sort the change she poured from her coin purse.

"That will do it, little lady. Your tiding is on its way, almost as fast as an angel could carry it."

Now Karin had to wait for the tiding of comfort to be delivered.

It was a few days later that Dad took the family out for pizza while Mother was at the hospital. Karin knew that he was trying to bring his own tiding of comfort to his family. After pizza, Dad stopped at the hospital.

"The doctor says that we can let you go visit Grandma as long as we don't stay too long."

That was the best news ever. They entered the automatic doors and found a world as busy as the mall, people coming and going with their Christmas packages. The elevator released them near the nurse's station, and Dad wound them around the hall to Grandmother's room. He opened the door to her room and with a gentle hand on Karin's shoulder, urged her to be the first to enter.

Karin took a hesitant step. Something about being in this strange place that held no tiding of comfort made her feel that any sound was too much. She practically held her breath and walked in.

There was her grandmother, almost sitting up. And covering her over the hospital sheets and blanket was the quilt.

"Come here, my little angel." Grandmother raised a weak hand in invitation.

"You got it. You got my tiding," Karin said exuberantly.

"Yes, my dear. It came this morning, and I have rested warm and comfortable underneath it ever since."

There were no visible angels in that room, but a softness and a peace not often known in hospitals before Christmas baptized everyone in it. Karin stood looking every bit like an angel who had delivered her message. And Grandmother, breathing easily, looked the part of one who had received a tiding of comfort for Christmas.

Oh, tidings of comfort and joy,

Comfort and joy

Oh, tidings of comfort and joy!

THE END

About the Author

Debbie Salter Goodwin attempted quilting only once. She would much rather piece words than quilts. However, she loves sleeping under them. Her life is much like a quilt pattern of very different squares. She was born in Texas and raised in Kansas City. She has served as children's director, taught speech and drama at a liberal arts college, and edited a teen magazine. For the past eighteen years, she has written a teen answer column for a Sunday school take-home paper.

Debbie has authored five books and multiple articles, and she speaks at retreats and conducts children's drama workshops. Besides supporting her pastor-husband in ministry, she directs an annual dessert theater and oversees other drama activities in her church.

Debbie lives in Chehalis, Washington, with her husband, Mark, daughter, Lisa, and a quilt in every room.

Additional copies of this book
are available from your local bookstore.

If you have enjoyed this book, or if it has
impacted your life, we would like to hear from you.
Please contact us at:
Honor Books
Department E
P.O. Box 55388
Tulsa, Oklahoma 74155

Or by e-mail at info@honorbooks.com